PLAY BALL!

The Math of **Sports**

Written by Bill Harrod

WORLD BOOK

www.worldbook.com

Co-published by agreement between Shi Tu Hui and World Book, Inc.

Shi Tu Hui
Room 1807, Block 1,
#3 West Dawang Road
Chaoyang District, Beijing 100025
P.R. China

World Book, Inc.
180 North LaSalle Street
Suite 900
Chicago, Illinois 60601
USA

© 2026. All rights reserved. This volume may not be reproduced in whole or in part in any form without prior written permission from the publisher.

WORLD BOOK and the GLOBE DEVICE are registered trademarks or trademarks of World Book, Inc.

Library of Congress Control Number: 2025942226

Aha! Academy: Math
ISBN: 978-0-7166-7377-4 (set, hardcover)

Play Ball! The Math of Sports
ISBN: 978-0-7166-7382-8 (hard cover)
ISBN: 978-0-7166-7445-0 (e-book)
ISBN: 978-0-7166-7435-1 (soft cover)

Staff

Editorial

Vice President
Tom Evans

Editorial Project Coordinator
Kaile Kilner

Senior Curriculum Designer
Caroline Davidson

Curriculum Designer
Mikayla Kightlinger

Proofreader
Nathalie Strassheim

Indexer
Nathaniel Lindstrom

Graphics and Design

Senior Visual
Communications Designer
Melanie Bender

Designer
Shannon Hagman

Written by Bill Harrod

Designed by Starletta Polster

Acknowledgments

The publishers gratefully acknowledge the following sources for photography. All illustrations were prepared by WORLD BOOK unless otherwise noted.

Cover: Abdul Razak Latif/Shutterstock; Benoit Daoust/Shutterstock; Lopolo/Shutterstock; Master1305/Shutterstock; JoeSAPhotos/Shutterstock

© Adam Stoltman/Alamy 7; Amazing Aerial/Alamy 24; © Bentley Archive/Popperfoto/Getty Images 35; © Geoff Marshall, Alamy 26; © Gado Images/Alamy 15; © Mark Pain, Alamy 10; © Sipa USA/Alamy 6; © Sportimage Ltd/Alamy 22; © Xiong Qi, Xinhua/Alamy 14; © Zoonar GmbH/Alamy 39, 48; © Focus on Sport/Getty Images Sport/Getty Images 21; © John W. McDonough/Sports Illustrated/Getty Images 20; © Stu Forster/Getty Images Sport/Getty Images 23; © Shutterstock 4, 5, 6, 7, 8, 9, 10, 11, 12, 13, 14, 15, 16, 17, 18, 19, 20, 21, 22, 23, 24, 25, 26, 27, 28, 29, 30, 31, 32, 33, 34, 35, 36, 37, 38, 39, 40, 41, 42, 43, 44, 45, 46, 47, 48

There is a glossary of terms on page 48. Terms defined in the glossary are in type that looks like *this* on their first appearance on any spread (two facing pages).

Contents

Introduction 4

① **Winning with statistics** 6
    Mean numbers 8
    Messi or Ronaldo? 10
    Numbers that don't fit in 12
    Gold medal graphs 14

② **What are the odds?** 16
    Finding success 18
    Managers taking their chances 20
    Rooting for the underdog 22

③ **Athletes using geometry** 24
    Where we play 26
    Balls, batons, and birdies 28
    Throwing things with math 30
    Space to play 32

④ **Fast math** 34
    Horses using math 36
    Car calculations 38
    Underwater math 40
    Tour de math 42

Go for the gold 44

Index 46

Glossary 48

Introduction

Athletes want to beat their opponents. Coaches want to win games. Fans want to prove that their favorite player is the greatest of all time. What can all these people use for victory? Math!

When you play or watch sports, you probably don't think much about math. But math is used in many ways in many sports. And not just for keeping score and timing athletes!

Read on to see how math helps athletes perform better, coaches make better decisions, and fans make better arguments.

Let the games begin!

Thanks, math, for making this pole vault possible!

Hay there! My favorite sport is actually stable tennis!

1 WINNING WITH STATISTICS

We can think of sports statistics as number facts about an athlete or team. Knowing how to find and use these math facts can help us better compare players and teams.

Who do you think is better?

We can use goal scoring and other statistics to help us see who is the best soccer player in the game today. Statistics can help us decide who was the greatest player in baseball, basketball, and other sports. We can use statistics from previous Olympics to help us predict how countries will do in future Olympics. The list of how statistics can be used in sports is endless!

Sports fans have a lot to argue about! Fans can debate about different players, teams, records, and much, much more. To help win their debate, fans often use *statistics*.

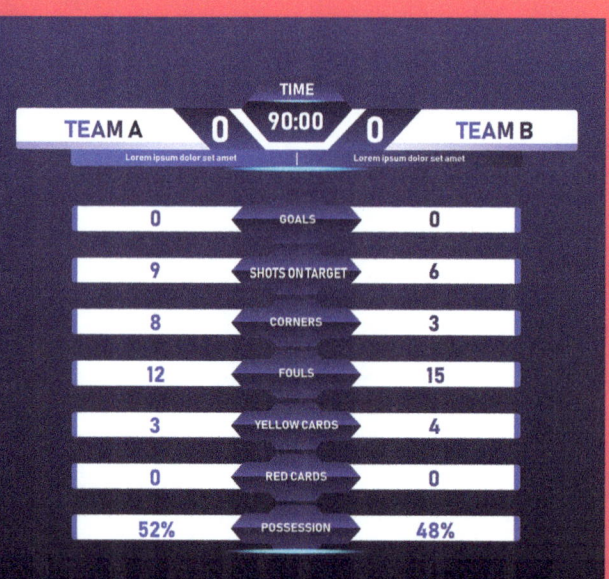

DID YOU KNOW?

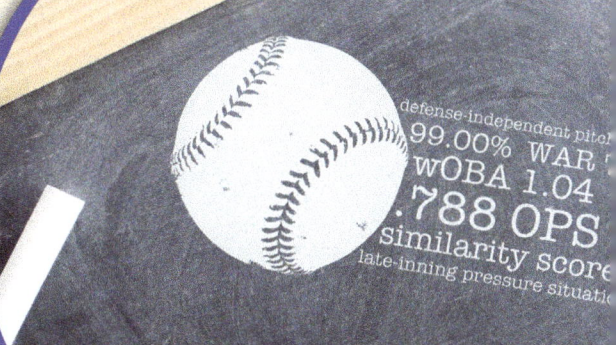

Sabermetrics is the study of baseball using statistics.

So, as you consider the debates you might have with your friends—Michael Jordan? or LeBron James? Lionel Messi or Cristiano Ronaldo? Real Madrid or FC Barcelona? Is Michael Phelps the greatest Olympian of all time?—consider how you could use statistics to help prove your point. Who knows, it might help you win your next debate!

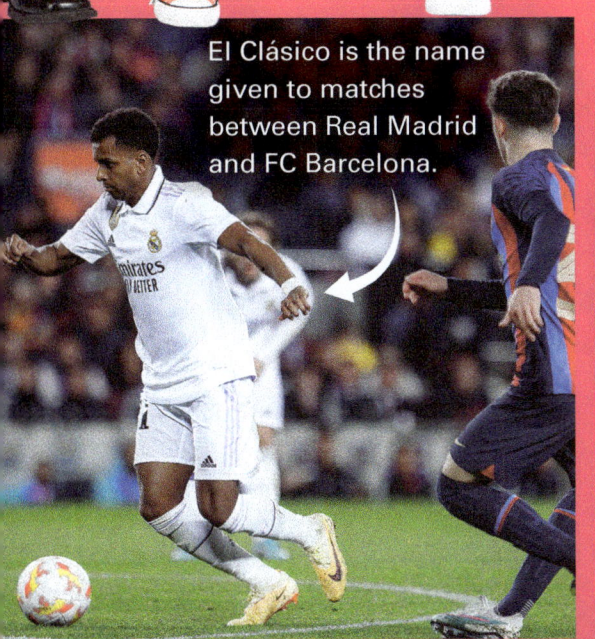

El Clásico is the name given to matches between Real Madrid and FC Barcelona.

Basketball fans have long debated who is the greatest basketball player of all time. Who do you think is the greatest?

No debate! I'm definitely the greatest!

Winning with statistics

Mean numbers

How many medals do you think China will win at the next Summer Olympics? To answer that question, you would want to first know how China has done at recent Olympics. Here are the number of medals China has won at the last five Summer Olympics:

Olympics	2008	2012	2016	2020	2024
Medals	100	92	70	89	92

China has won more gold medals in Olympic table tennis than all other countries combined! And it's not close!

OK, so we've got a group of numbers here. How can we use these to help us try to figure out how many medals China usually wins? **Statistics** to the rescue!

What one number do you think best represents all the numbers in the table? Three you can choose from are the *mean*, *median*, and *mode*. The mean and median are usually considered better than the mode (don't take it personally, mode!). So, we will just use mean and median going forward. You can check how to calculate these in the box on the next page!

China has won more Olympic medals in diving than any other sport.

How are you supposed to make sense of a large group of numbers? Let's replace a bunch of numbers with just one!

Averages

Mean
The sum of the numbers in the group divided by how many numbers are in the group.

Median
The middle value in a group of numbers arranged in numerical order. If there are an even number of numbers, then we take the mean of the two numbers in the middle.

Mode
The value that occurs most frequently.

The table has a mean of 88.6 and a median of 92. Some people might prefer the mean. Others might prefer the median. In this case, it really doesn't matter because they're close. From the data, we see that China has recently won about 90 medals at each Summer Olympics. So, we can predict that China will win about 90 medals at the next Summer Olympics.

CAREER CORNER

If you enjoy math, you may want to consider becoming a statistician! Statisticians are people who collect, analyze, and interpret data using statistical methods. They work in such diverse fields as business, education, health and medicine, insurance, and surveys.

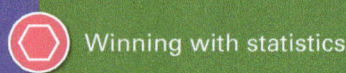

Winning with statistics

Messi or Ronaldo?

Let's start by using goals scored as a way of comparison. Both Messi and Ronaldo played in La Liga (Spain's top soccer league) from 2009 to 2018. Here are the number of goals they scored each season:

Season	Messi (Barcelona)	Ronaldo (Real Madrid)
2009-2010	34	26
2010-2011	31	40
2011-2012	50	46
2012-2013	46	34
2013-2014	28	31
2014-2015	43	48
2015-2016	26	35
2016-2017	37	25
2017-2018	34	26

Messi had a *mean* of 36.6 and a *median* of 34. Ronaldo had a mean of 34.6 and a median of 34. Does that help us decide who is better? Well, no, the means are close and the medians are the same!

Messi helped lead Argentina to the 2022 World Cup championship.

Are you a soccer fan? Who do you think is a better soccer player, Lionel Messi or Cristiano Ronaldo? We can use *statistics* to help us out!

However, there is more to being a great soccer player than just scoring a lot of goals. What other statistics could we use to compare the two? Here are a few individual and team accomplishments to consider:

Accomplishment (through 2023)	Lionel Messi	Cristiano Ronaldo
Won Ballon d'Or (world's best player)	8	5
Named La Liga's best player	9	1
Team won domestic league title	12	7
Team won Champions League (annual tournament of world's best soccer clubs)	4	5

OK, now it looks like stats might help us out! It appears that Messi might be better. Do you agree? Are there other stats we should consider?

Ronaldo has scored more international goals than anybody else in soccer history.

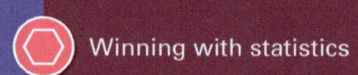

Winning with statistics

Numbers that don't fit in

Most countries win about the same number of medals each time they compete in the Olympics. But, sometimes, strange things happen! The number of medals the United States won in the Summer Olympics from 1984 to 2000 was:

Olympics	1984	1988	1992	1996	2000
Medals	174	94	108	101	93

The 1984 figure looks out of place, doesn't it? Because many top athletes from other countries didn't compete in the Olympics that year, the United States won more medals than normal.

Calculating the *mean* and the *median* with and without the "174" figure, you get:

With "174" — Mean = 114, Median = 101

Without "174" — Mean = 99, Median = 98

Notice that the outlier caused the mean to change more than the median. Outliers affect the mean more than the median.

The first recorded **Olympic Games** took place in 776 B.C. at Olympia in western Greece. The only event was the stadion, a running race of 192 meters (210 yards).

Sometimes, when we see a list of numbers, one value doesn't fit in with its friends. A number like this that is much higher or lower than the others in the list is called an *outlier*.

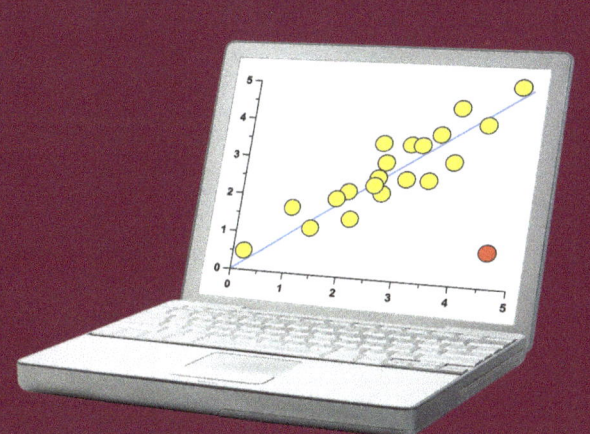

Different sports have ways to control for outliers in scoring. In both figure skating and gymnastics, a group of judges score the athlete's performance. The highest and lowest scores are tossed, and the remaining scores are used to determine the competitor's final score. Dropping the highest and lowest scores helps control for a judge giving an outlier score.

In diving, seven judges evaluate each performance. The two highest and two lowest scores are tossed, and the final score is determined from the remaining three scores.

In some snowboarding events the lowest run score is dropped, so that one bad result (outlier) doesn't prevent an athlete from winning.

13

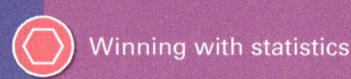
Winning with statistics

Gold medal graphs

Let's see who were the leading medal winners at the 2022 Winter Olympic Games in Beijing, China.

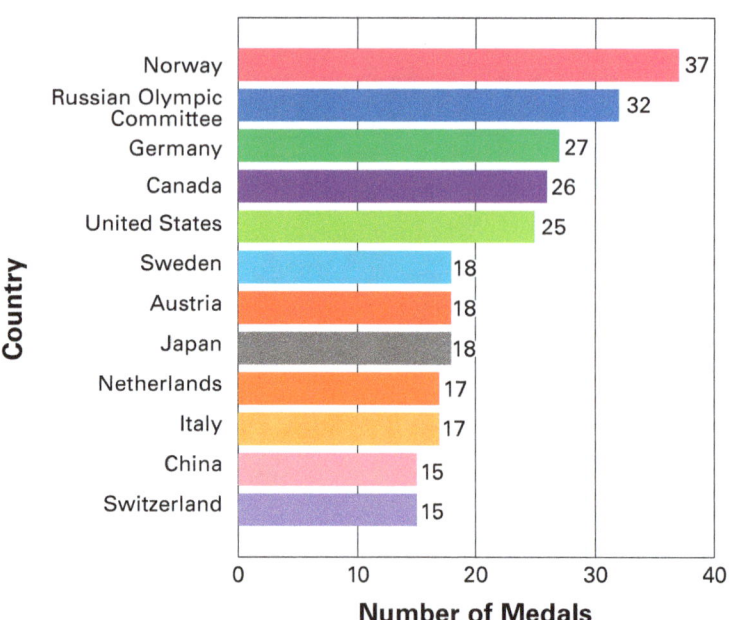

This first graph is a bar graph. Each bar shows how many medals the 12 leading countries won. We can easily see which country won the most medals (uff da, it's Norway!) and compare the leading nations. For example, we see that both China and Switzerland won the same number of medals—15.

Chinese American freestyle skier Eileen Gu won two gold medals and one silver medal at the 2022 Winter Olympic Games.

While on the internet, you see a table of medal winners from the 2022 Winter Olympics. Is there an easier way to compare the countries? How about using *graphs*?

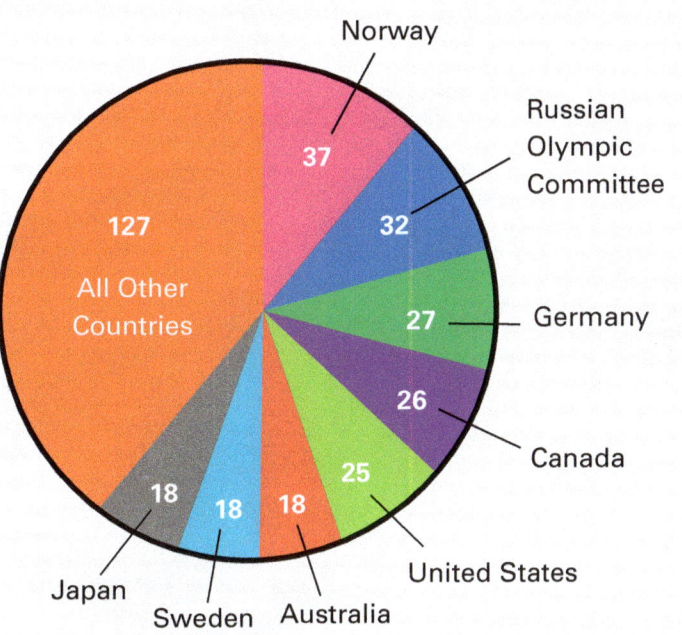

The second graph is called a circle graph (or pie chart). Each wedge represents a country or group of countries. In this graph, the size of the wedge is proportional to the number of medals won. Interesting! The graph shows that the leading eight countries won more medals than all other countries combined! You wouldn't have known that looking at a table.

These two graphs show the same information, but you might prefer one over the other. The bar graph is probably easier to read. But, the pie graph allows you to compare the leading countries with all of the other countries.

CURIOUS CONNECTIONS

MEDICINE Graphs can save lives! During the Crimean War (1853-1856), British nurse Florence Nightingale made a graph showing that many deaths in British Army hospitals were caused by poor sanitary conditions. Nightingale and her famous graph led to many worldwide hospital reforms which have saved countless lives!

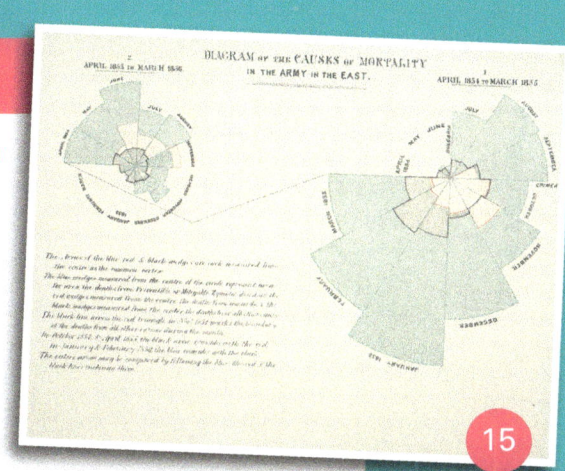

2

WHAT ARE THE ODDS?

In sports, we often want to know the chances of success. The chances a team wins today's game or the championship. The chances a basketball player makes a free throw. The chances a softball player gets a hit.

Let's use the math I taught you in class!

There are ten seconds left in the basketball game, and your team is winning by one point. Wait, what's going on here? The coach just took out the best player and replaced him with someone else! Maybe he's using *probabilities* and *percentages!*

Probabilities and percentages give

us that information. Probabilities and percentages are similar numbers. For example, probabilities tell us what are the chances a basketball player makes his next free throw. Percentages tell us how many free throws he makes for every 100 attempts.

We can easily go back and forth between the two. To change a percentage into a probability, divide the percentage by 100. To change a probability to a percentage, do the opposite and multiply the number by 100.

What are the odds?

Finding success

To find the probability of an event happening, we use the formula:

$$P = \frac{\text{favorable outcomes}}{\text{total outcomes}}$$

By "favorable outcomes," we mean the outcomes that we are looking for.

For example, when you roll a die, there are 6 possible outcomes: 1, 2, 3, 4, 5, and 6. How could we find the probability of rolling a "1" or a "6"? Well, out of the 6 possible outcomes, two of them (the "1" and the "6") are favorable to us. So, the probability is:

$$P = \frac{2}{6} = .33 \text{ or } 33\%$$

Ancient Roman dice found at Pompeii, a city destroyed in 79 B.C. by the eruption of Mount Vesuvius

(Quick reminder: 2 divided by 6 = .33, and to convert .33 to a *percentage*, we just multiply it by 100 to get 33%)

If you want to find the chances of success, you are going to need to know how to find *probabilities*. Probabilities tell you how likely it is that a certain outcome will happen.

Let's look at a sports example.

Table tennis became an Olympic sport in 1988. Between 1988 and 2024, China won 37 gold medals out of the 42 that were awarded (singles, doubles, team). What percentage of the gold medals did they win during that time?

$$p = \frac{37}{42} = .88 = 88\%$$

In these examples we are finding the probability or percentage of one event happening. We could also find the probability of multiple events happening, for example tossing three coins that all land heads. These compound probabilities can be found, but the math is a little trickier.

DID YOU KNOW?

When calculating probability problems with dice, we assume that each die is fair—that is, that each of the six numbers has an equal chance of being rolled. Dice can be "loaded" so that one number is rolled more frequently than the others. Archaeologists have found loaded dice from many ancient civilizations.

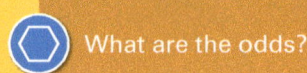 What are the odds?

Managers taking their chances

Some baseball players hit better against right-handed pitchers than left-handed pitchers (or vice versa). Managers use information like this to help them decide who to start, when to change pitchers, and when to use pinch-hitters. Basketball coaches use probabilities when they put in better free-throw shooters at the end of a close game.

Shaquille O'Neal was a great basketball player, but a lousy free-throw shooter. Some coaches took advantage of this by using a "Hack-a-Shaq" strategy of intentionally fouling O'Neal in critical situations. They figured there was a better chance of O'Neal missing free throws than of his team missing shots. Of course, opponents couldn't do that the whole game because all of their players would quickly foul out.

How do coaches and managers decide who to play in a game? They often use *probabilities* to help them decide which players give the team the best chance of winning!

Here is something many people struggle with: probabilities do not tell you EXACTLY how many times an event will happen. For example, if you flip a coin 100 times you should get about 50 heads. That doesn't mean that you will always get exactly 50 heads. But you should get a number close to 50.

Basketball legend Larry Bird hit about 90% of his free throws. Does that mean that Bird always hit 9 free throws in a row and then missed the tenth? Nope! Did he always make 9 out of every 10 free throws? Nope! It means that he usually made around 9 free throws for every 10 he attempted.

CAREER CORNER

What does it mean when a meteorologist says there is a 90% chance of rain in your city tomorrow? It does not mean (1) that 90% of the city will get rain tomorrow or (2) that it will rain for 90% of the time tomorrow. It does mean that there is a 90% chance that a specific location in the city will get rain sometime tomorrow.

What are the odds?

Rooting for the underdog

Some sports have single-game playoffs, where whoever wins the game advances to the next round. Other sports have playoff series where the first team to win two out of three games wins the series. Other playoff series are best 3-out-of-5 or best 4-out-of-7.

Let's say that English soccer clubs Manchester United and Liverpool meet in a series of matches. Assume that Man U has a 65% chance of winning a match (sorry, Liverpool) and that there are no ties. How likely is Manchester United to win the series?

The chance each team wins the series is:

Series length	Manchester United wins series	Liverpool wins series
1 game	65.0%	35.0%
Best 2-out-of-3	71.8%	28.2%
Best 3-out-of-5	76.5%	23.5%
Best 4-out-of-7	80.0%	20.0%

It doesn't matter how long a playoff series is, the better team has the same chance of winning the series. Right? Actually, no! Using compound *probabilities,* we can see why!

As you see from the table, the longer the series, the more likely that the favored team (Man U) wins. The better team prefers a longer series because the more games it plays, the more its advantage works in its favor, and the more likely it is to win the series.

So, don't be surprised when the better team loses in a single-game playoff—for example, in the knockout round of the World Cup soccer tournament. In these tournaments there are bound to be upsets.

CURIOUS CONNECTIONS

GENETICS To find the *percentages* in the table, we used compound probabilities. Geneticists (people who study heredity) use compound probabilities to find the chances that characteristics are passed from one generation to the next.

3 ATHLETES USING GEOMETRY

In basketball, as in other sports, the size of the court and the size and shape of the equipment matters. When you shoot a basketball, does it matter at what direction *(angle)* you shoot the ball? Of course it does! Wait a minute! *Geometry* is the study of shapes, sizes (called *areas*), angles, and more. Maybe, geometry can help us with sports!

My teacher was right about math being useful!

Imagine trying to play a game of basketball on a court the size of a soccer field. With a ball *shaped* like a *cube*! Obviously, this wouldn't work!

It's Hammer (Throw) Time!

Want to find the fastest way to run around a track? Use geometry! Want help throwing a discus, hammer, or javelin far? Use geometry! Can geometry help pole vaulters? Yep, them, too! Can geometry help you run as fast as an Olympian can? Uh, no, for that you'll have to practice.

And, it's not just track and field that uses geometry! Geometry is used in such diverse sports as badminton and baseball, hockey and (horse) polo, and sailing and sumo wrestling!

So, read on to find out how geometry is used in the wide world of sports!

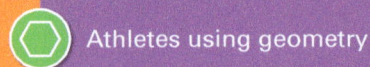
Athletes using geometry

Where we play

Have you ever played badminton, basketball, soccer, tennis, or volleyball? What do all of their fields and courts have in common? They're all rectangles. Most sports are played on rectangular surfaces.

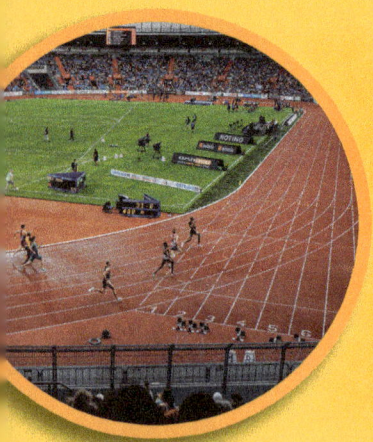

However, some sports, like cricket and Australian rules football, are designed to be played on an oval-shaped field. Racetracks for cars, horses, and runners are also often oval-shaped, because it is easier to turn going around an oval than around a rectangle.

Hockey rinks are basically rectangular, but their corners are curved. The curved corners keep the game moving because the puck can't get stuck in the corners.

Different sports play on differently shaped fields. The *shape* of the field often depends on how the sport is played. Let's see some different shapes that are important to sports!

Loser buys dinner!

Sumo wrestlers compete in a circular ring.

Shapes are not just important to fields and courts. Let's see where else shapes are important in sports!

The boats in sailing competitions often have triangular sails. These sails allow the boat to go faster than rectangular-shaped sails would allow.

In archery, competitors shoot arrows at a circular target. Archers get more points the closer their arrow lands to the center.

27

Athletes using geometry

Balls, batons, and birdies

Sports balls come in different sizes. The smallest balls, the ones used in ping pong and squash, each have **circumferences** of about 12.5 centimeters. Basketballs have a circumference of about 75 centimeters. You could fit over 200 squash balls inside a basketball!

Look closely at the soccer ball. Do you notice two shapes? A soccer ball is made up of 12 pentagons (5-sided figures) and 20 hexagons (6-sided figures).

Other sports have differently shaped equipment.

Hockey pucks are *cylinders*. One reason for using a cylinder and not a ball is that it is easier for hockey players to control a puck than a ball. Also, pucks are more likely than balls to stay on the ice. However, as you see in this photo, pucks can get airborne and do occasionally fly into the stands!

Most sports use perfectly round balls. In *geometry*, these round balls are called *spheres*. Some sports, like football, use balls with different *shapes*.

Badminton shuttlecocks are *cones* (mostly, they are not pointed at the end). Shuttlecocks are designed so that they turn when they are hit. That way the rubber base, and not the feathers, is hit on each shot.

The batons used in relay races are hollow cylinders. They are shaped this way to make them lightweight, easy to pass, and easy to run with.

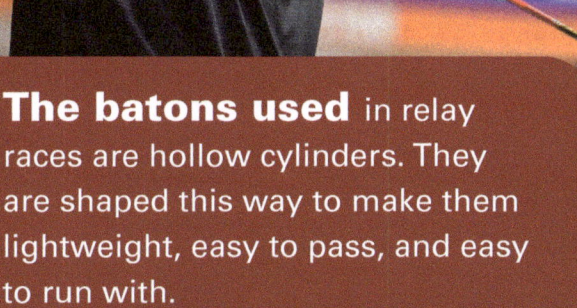

DID YOU KNOW?

What is the shape of a football or rugby ball (seen to the left)? They are called prolate spheroids. Spheroids are solid figures that resemble a sphere but are not perfectly round. Prolate spheroids are longer than they are wide.

29

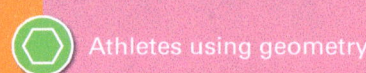
Athletes using geometry

Throwing things with math

Angles are especially important in track and field. Javelin throwers have found that they can get maximum distance if they throw the javelin at about a 35° angle. Athletes who throw the discus, hammer, or shot put try to throw these at about a 40° angle. The best pole vaulters usually have a takeoff angle of about 20°.

Other sports use angles, too! Bowlers use angles when they knock pins into each other. Billiards players use angles when they knock the balls into the pockets. Volleyball players use angles when directing the ball to the setting *area* and when spiking the ball.

Remember learning about *angles* in school? Athletes learned about them in school, too. And now, they use angles to help themselves win!

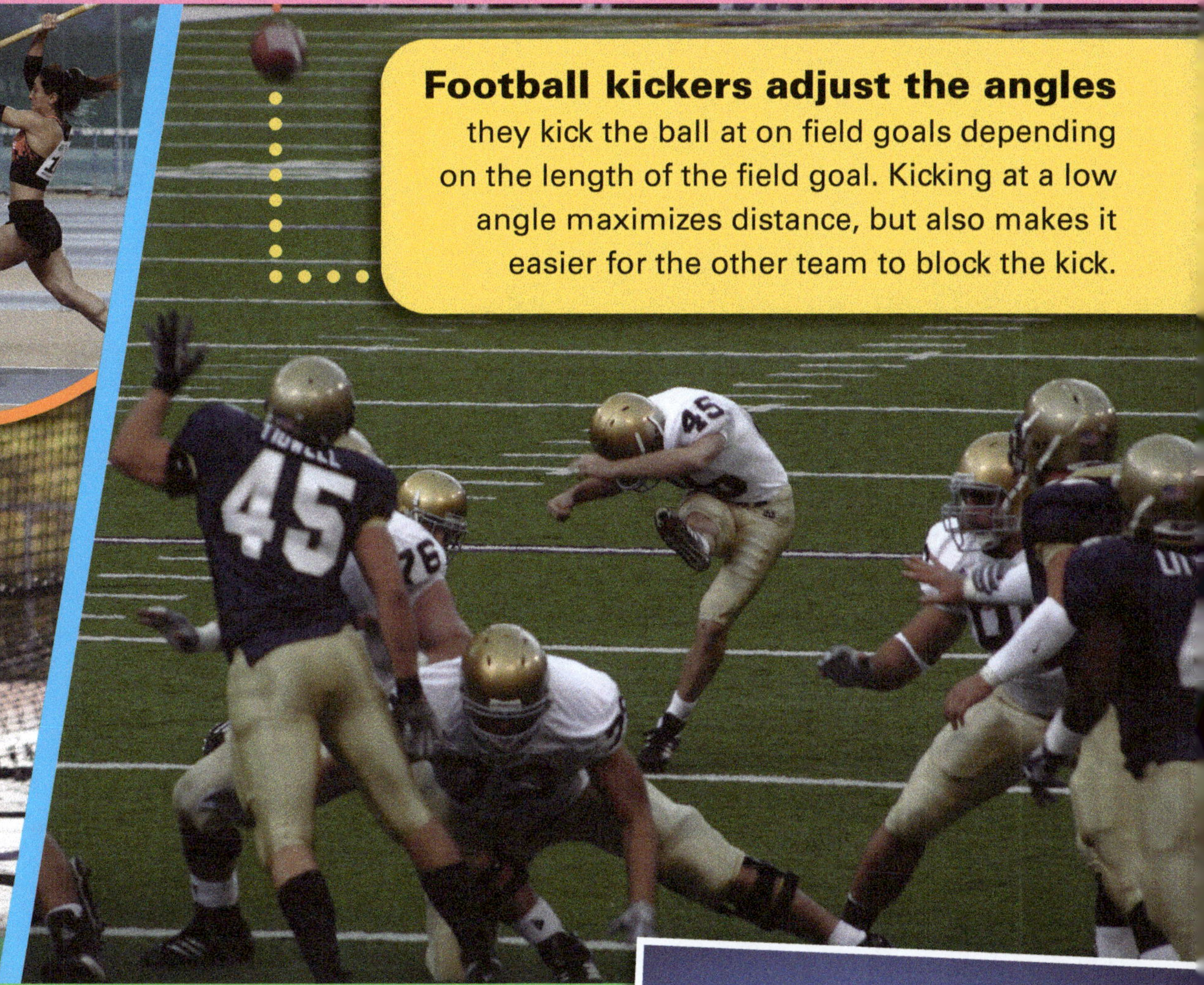

Football kickers adjust the angles they kick the ball at on field goals depending on the length of the field goal. Kicking at a low angle maximizes distance, but also makes it easier for the other team to block the kick.

CURIOUS CONNECTIONS

ASTRONOMY Astronomers use angles to find how far away stars are from Earth using parallax. Parallax is the angle between the straight lines that join a star or another space object to different points of observation.

Athletes using geometry

Space to play

Let's start with badminton. The singles court is 17 feet wide and 22 feet long. We can multiply these **dimensions** together to find the **area** of 374 ft². The doubles court is 22 ft x 20 ft, so its area is 440 ft². If each doubles player covers half the court, that means each player is responsible for covering 220 ft².

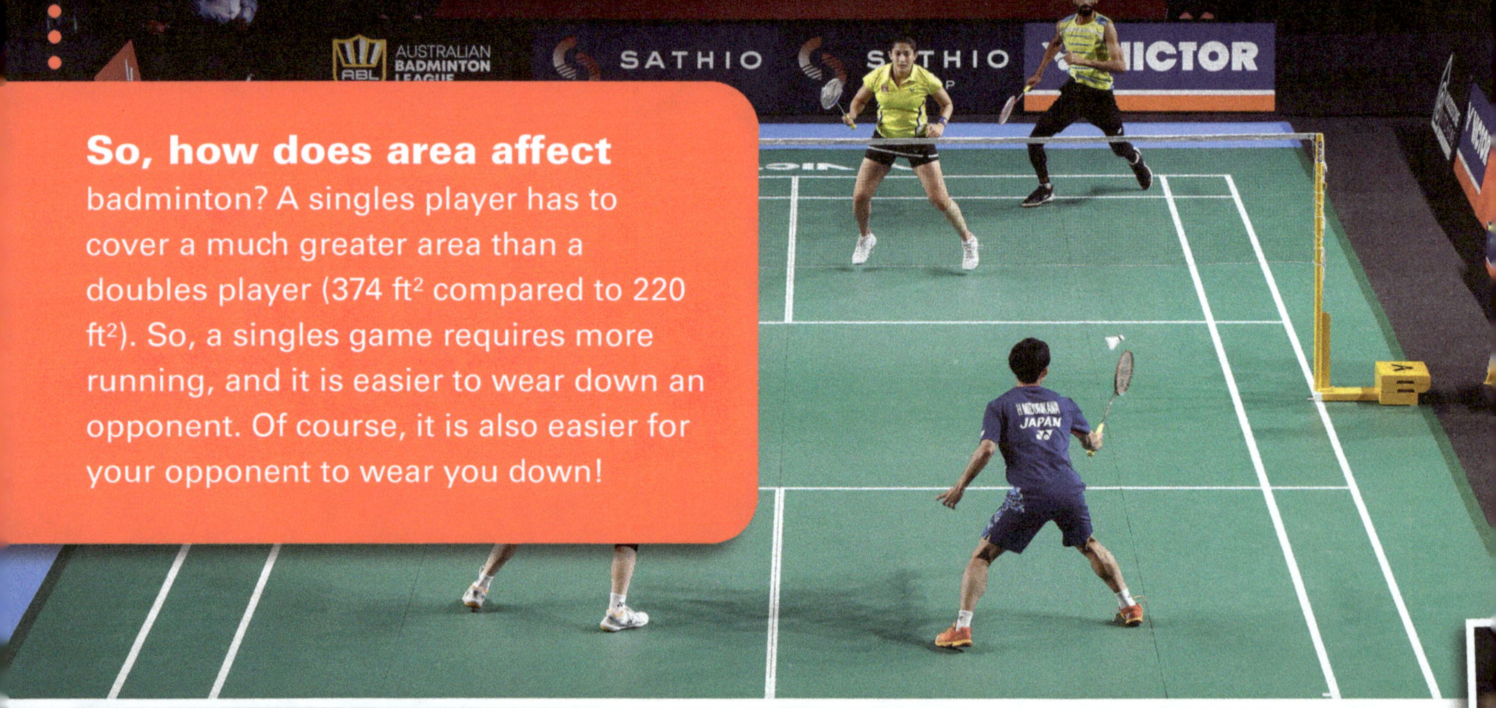

So, how does area affect badminton? A singles player has to cover a much greater area than a doubles player (374 ft² compared to 220 ft²). So, a singles game requires more running, and it is easier to wear down an opponent. Of course, it is also easier for your opponent to wear you down!

Which sport do you think has the largest playing field? The picture to the left probably gave the answer away... the answer is polo. (Horse polo, not water polo.) A polo field is usually 900 feet by 480 feet. By comparison, you could fit over 950 badminton courts on a polo field with room to spare!

Wait until you see me playing badminton!

All sports play on some sort of field or court. Does the size of the field or court matter? Read on to find out!

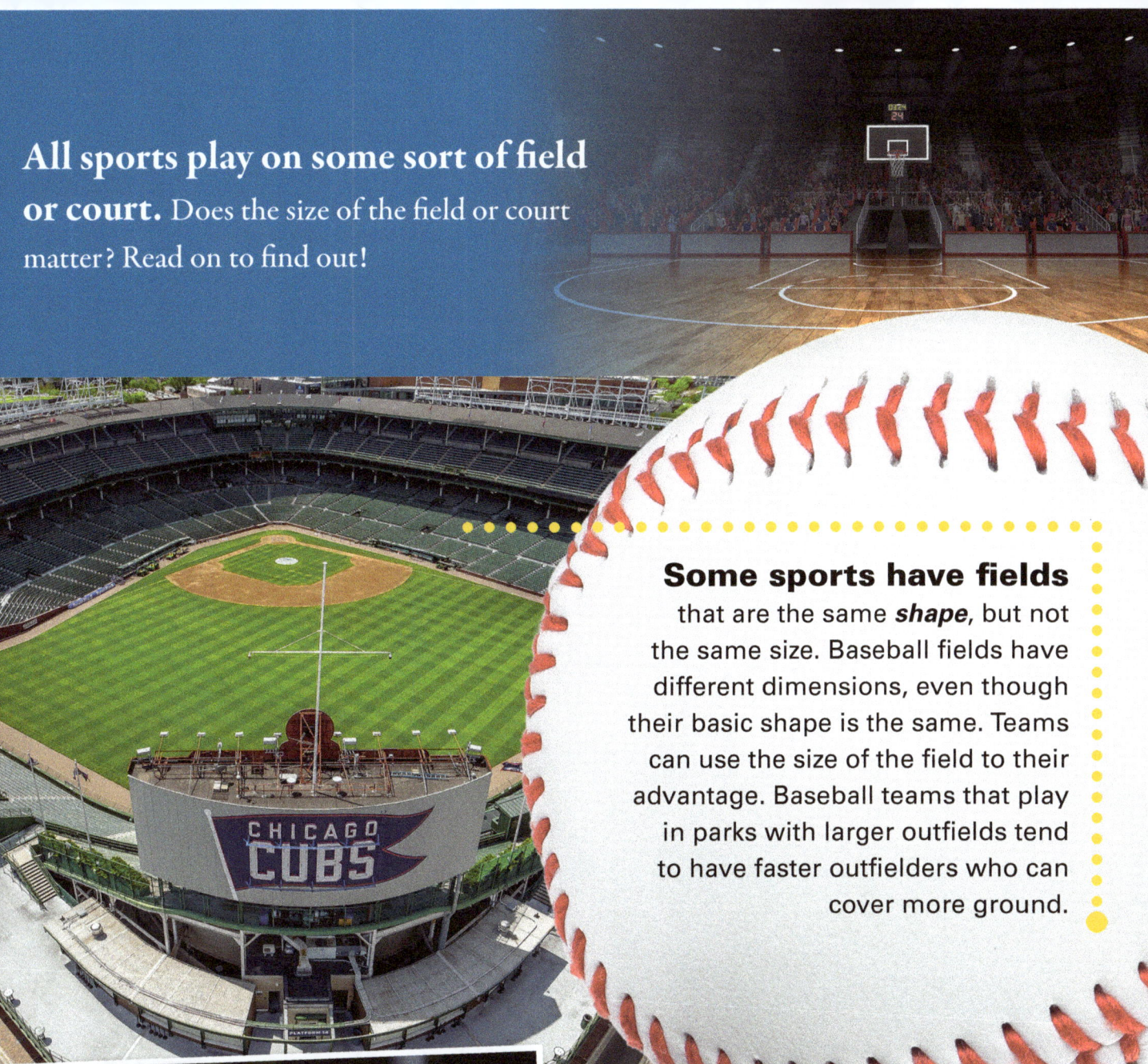

Some sports have fields that are the same *shape*, but not the same size. Baseball fields have different dimensions, even though their basic shape is the same. Teams can use the size of the field to their advantage. Baseball teams that play in parks with larger outfields tend to have faster outfielders who can cover more ground.

For centuries, Native Americans have played a sport called **stickball,** which is similar to the modern sport of lacrosse (seen to the left). In the past, each team could have hundreds, and possibly over a thousand, players who played on a field that could be a mile or more long!

FAST MATH

Do you ever compete with your friends to see who can bike, run, or swim the fastest? However people race, math is important. In a race, athletes see who can go a certain distance in the shortest amount of time. Math is needed to measure both distance and time. If you know how much time it takes an athlete to cover a certain distance, you can calculate their speed. That's math, too!

The Boston Marathon. The Monaco Grand Prix. The Indianapolis 500. The Kentucky Derby. The Tour de France. Races make up some of the world's most popular and exciting sporting events!

In 1954, British runner **Roger Bannister** became the first person to run a mile in under four minutes. If you want to run a four-minute mile, you need to average running about 15 miles (24 kilometers) per hour ... and keep that pace going for four whole minutes!

Math is used various ways to help athletes find ways to go faster. Need to design bikes and cars to go fast? Math can help with that! Need strategies to get around a racetrack as quick as possible? Math can do that, too!

Make sure you don't race through these pages. You might miss something interesting!

Fast math

Horses using math

Imagine drawing two circles, one with a **radius** of 10 centimeters and another with a radius of 20 centimeters. When you unroll the circles, the 10-centimeter circle is shorter than the 20-centimeter circle. What does that have to do with track? Imagine having two (highly trained!) ants walk around each circle. Who would win? The ant walking around the 10-centimeter circle has a shorter distance, so it should win. Right?

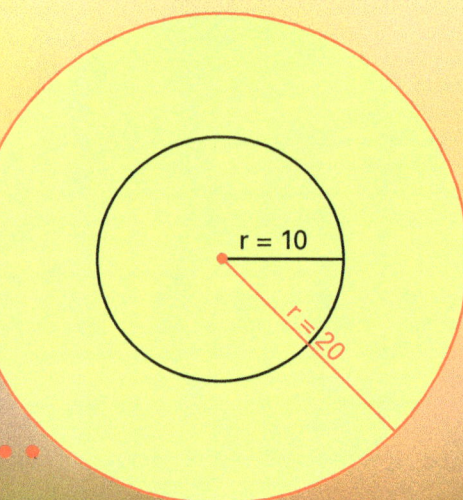

Learning math made me brilli-ant!

The same basic idea works in running. Runners often run around an oval, which is similar to a circle. The farther a runner is from the center, the larger an oval she must run around. To make sure that all runners run an equal distance, the runners on the outside lanes get what appears to be a head start. Actually, the track has been measured out so that all runners run the same length.

Have you ever watched a race and wondered why some runners seem to have a head start? That seems unfair, doesn't it? However, there is a mathematical reason that runners line up this way!

Horses also know this! (Well, at least their jockeys do.) In horse racing, horses often run on the inside of the track. By staying as far inside as possible, they don't have as far to run and can finish the race faster!

Hippodromes were places for **horse and chariot races** in ancient Greece and Rome. The largest hippodrome in ancient Rome was the oval-shaped Circus Maximus, which seated about 250,000 spectators! No modern-day stadium comes close to that figure!

We came! We raced! We won!

No, this is not an actual photo from ancient Rome! It's from a modern-day festival.

37

 Fast math

Car calculations

In a sport where every second counts, racing teams use math and science (which itself is partially based on math) to get every advantage they can. Cars are designed so that they can move through the air as quickly and *efficiently* as possible. Crews find ways to minimize pit stop times. Drivers use various strategies to maximize fuel efficiency.

Banked turns are ones where the track is tilted so that the top of the track is higher than the bottom. Cars can travel faster around banked turns than around level turns.

Drivers also use math to find the best way to drive around turns. While they usually try to stay close to the center of the track, sometimes it is faster to drive on the outside of the track! For example, if a track has banked turns, drivers can often travel faster if they drive closer to the top of the turns.

Cars travel for hundreds of miles in an auto race. Yet, the difference between winning and losing is often determined by mere seconds, or even less!

There are many different types of cars used in racing. Here are the approximate top speeds for three different types of races:

- Drag Racing (340 mph/550 kph)
- Indianapolis 500 (240 mph/390 kph)
- NASCAR (200 mph/320 kph)

Drag racing cars travel much faster because they race in a straight line for only a short distance. They travel so fast that they need a parachute to help slow them down!

🖱️ TECH TIME

Car racing teams can use wind tunnels to check their car's performance. Wind tunnels show how air flows around the car. Racing teams design cars to cut through the air easily so that the cars are faster and more fuel efficient.

Fast math

Underwater math

Swimmers do everything they can to swim as fast as possible. They focus on their technique and look for anything that might be slowing them down. They learn how many strokes it takes them to swim each lap so that they go through the water as quickly and *efficiently* as possible. They pace their stroke lengths and stamina. Math can help in all these areas.

When swimmers come to the end of the pool, they do a flip turn so that they can do the next lap. They must pace themselves correctly so they can turn as quickly as possible.

What's a swimmer's favorite kind of math? Dive-ision!

These swimmers jump backwards to start a backstroke race.

We've seen how math can be used on land. It can also be used in water! Let's see how swimmers can use math to help themselves win races and Olympic medals!

Do seconds or even parts of a second matter to swimmers? Yes! To the right are the winning times for the 100-meter women's freestyle gold medal race at the Summer Olympic Games from 1952 to 2024. What do you notice about the *graph*?

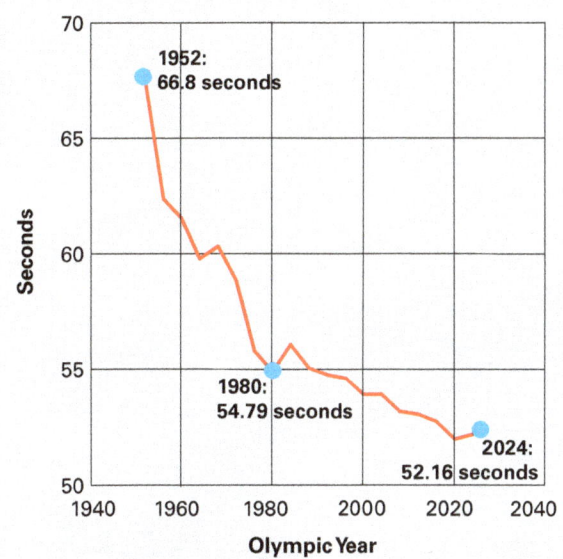

100-Meter Women's Freestyle Winning Times at the Summer Olympics

- 1952: 66.8 seconds
- 1980: 54.79 seconds
- 2024: 52.16 seconds

As you see from the graph, from 1952 to 2024, swimmers are getting faster! From 1952 to 1980, the winning time decreased by about 12 seconds. Since 1980, the winning time has decreased by less than 3 seconds! So, while the time is still going down, it is now decreasing at a more gradual rate. Mathematicians can use a graph like this to predict what time will win the race in future Olympics.

DID YOU KNOW?

American swimmer Michael Phelps has won more medals (28) and more gold medals (23) than any other athlete in Olympic Games history. As of 2024, Phelps has won more than twice as many gold medals as any other Olympian!

Fast math

Tour de **math**

Like automobile racers, bicyclists use math to race as fast as possible. Bicycles are designed so that they can move through the air as quickly and *efficiently* as possible. In the Tour de France, cyclists race in teams. Teams develop racing strategies that allow one cyclist to race for the championship while his teammates support him. One strategy that cyclists use is "drafting." Drafting is when one cyclist rides close behind another to reduce wind resistance. That way, the cyclist in the back isn't using as much energy.

Bicyclists also test in wind tunnels to help find ways to travel faster.

Some bicycle races are held on an oval track. Similar to running and horse racing, bicyclists try to ride as close to the center as possible to go faster around the track.

Do you enjoy bicycling? Imagine racing over 3,000 kilometers in about three weeks! Sometimes climbing mountains! Welcome to the Tour de France, one of the world's most demanding sporting events. Let's see how math can help!

BMX races are another popular form of bicycle racing. BMX races are held on dirt tracks that have many bumps and sharp turns. The cyclists ride bicycles that have small wheels and wide tires to help prevent them from slipping in the turns. Math is used to design tracks for BMX races.

TECH TIME

Technological advances in equipment over the years have helped athletes perform better. The bicycles used in cycling events in today's Olympics are more advanced than the bicycles used in the first modern Olympic Games of 1896 and allow cyclists to go much faster.

43

Go for gold!

You will need:
- Paper
- Pencil
- Stopwatch
- Calculator
- Ruler
- Place to run

Give it a try

1. Make a race track with a start line and a finish line. It doesn't matter how long the course is as long as everyone runs the same distance. To make it easier to keep track of time, have only one person run at a time.
2. Make a chart to record each person's time.

Person	Time (seconds)

3. As each person runs the race, record their times on the chart.
4. Have one of your friends record your time running the race.

The first recorded Olympic Games consisted of one event, a running race. You can hold your own Olympics with your friends! Medal ceremony optional.

You three are racing for second place!

Let's see if you can keep up with me this time!

Try this next!

Now it's stats time!
- Calculate the mean and median for the runners' times. You can flip to pages 8-9 to remind yourself how means and medians are calculated.
- Make a bar graph of the times. A ruler will make it easier to draw straight lines.
- What *percentage* of the runners ran faster (or slower) than you? You can flip to pages 18-19 to remind yourself how percentages are calculated.

This activity can be extended to a swimming, bicycling, or any other type of race. You could hold your own neighborhood Olympics with multiple events!

QUESTION TIME!

Did anybody have an *outlier* time? If so, how did that time affect the mean and median of the times? Based on your data, if you were to run a race against a random person, what are the chances you would win? If you and your friends ran on a circular track, are there any strategies you could use to help you win?

Index

A

angles, 24, 30-31
archery, 27
area, 24, 30, 32
astronomy, 31
averages, 9

B

badminton, 26, 29, 32
Bannister, Roger, 35
baseball, 7, 20, 33
basketball, 16-17, 20-21, 24, 26, 28
batons, 29
bicycling, 35, 42-43
billiards, 30
Bird, Larry, 21
birdies. *See* shuttlecocks
BMX racing, 43
bowling, 30

C

cars, racing, 26, 35, 38-39
circles, 15, 27, 36, 45
circumference, 28
coin flips, 19, 21
compound probabilities, 19, 23
cones, 29
cylinders, 28-29

D

dice, 18-19

dimensions, 32-33
diving, 8, 13

E

efficiency, 38-40, 42

F

football, 26, 29, 31

G

genetics, 23
geometry, 24-33
graphs, 14-15, 41, 45
Gu, Eileen, 14
gymnastics, 12

H

hexagons, 28
hippodromes, 37
hockey, 26, 28
horses, 26, 32, 36-37

J

javelin throwing, 30

L

lacrosse, 33
loaded dice, 19

M

mean, 8-10, 12, 45

46

median, 8-10, 12, 45
Messi, Lionel, 10-11
meteorology, 21
mode, 8-9

N
Nightingale, Florence, 15

O
Olympic Games, 8-9, 12-15, 19, 41, 43, 45
O'Neal, Shaquille, 20
outliers, 12-13, 45
ovals, 26, 36-37, 42

P
parallax, 31
pentagons, 28
percentages, 16-19, 22-23, 45
Phelps, Michael, 41
ping pong. *See* table tennis
pole vaulting, 5, 30
probabilities, 16-23

R
radius, 36
rectangles, 26
Ronaldo, Cristiano, 10-11
running, 13, 25-26, 29, 32, 35-37, 44-45

S
sabermetrics, 7
shuttlecocks, 29
skating, 12
snowboarding, 13
soccer, 10-11, 22-23, 26, 28
spheres, 29
spheroids, 29
statistics, 6-15
stickball, 33
swimming, 40-41

T
table tennis, 8, 19, 28
tennis, 26
Tour de France, 42-43

V
volleyball, 26, 30

W
wind tunnels, 39, 42

Glossary

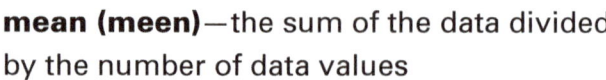

angle (ANG guhl)—a figure formed by two lines that meet at a point

area (AIR ee uh)—the space inside a flat shape

circumference (suhr KUHM fuhr uhns)—the distance around the boundary of a circle

cone (kohn)—a solid shape; it has a flat, round base and narrows to a point at the top

cube (kyoob)—a solid shape with six square faces or sides, all equal

cylinder (SIHL uhn duhr)—a solid shape; its ends are two equal circles

dimension (duh MEHN shuhn)—a measurement of length, breadth, or thickness

efficient (uh FIHSH uhnt)—able to produce the effect wanted without waste of time or energy

geometry (jee OM uh tree)—the branch of mathematics that involves the study of the shape, size, and positions of lines, angles, curves, and figures

graph (graf, grahf)—a drawing that shows the relative sizes of numerical data

mean (meen)—the sum of the data divided by the number of data values

median (MEE dee uhn)—the value in the middle when the data is listed from least to greatest

mode (mohd)—the most common value in a data set

outlier (owt LY uhr)—an unusually large or small data value compared to the others

percentage (puhr SEHN tihj)—a rate or proportion of each hundred; part of each hundred

probability (PROB uh BIHL uh tee)—the branch of mathematics that deals with the chances of different possible outcomes of random events

radius (RAY dee uhs)—any line going straight from the center to the edge of a circle or sphere

shape (shayp)—the outward outline of an object; form; figure

sphere (sfihr)—a perfectly round solid shape

statistics (stuh TIHS tihks)—the branch of mathematics that deals with collecting and analyzing data

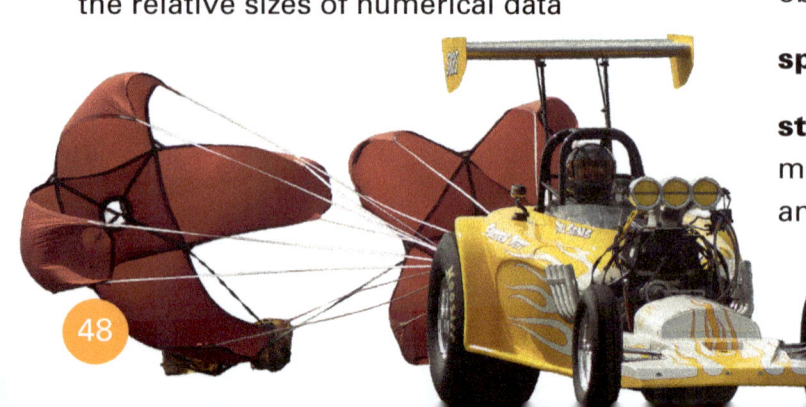

48